Animal Homes

A Hermit Crab's Shell

Arthur Best

Cavendish Square

New York

Published in 2019 by Cavendish Square Publishing, LLC
243 5th Avenue, Suite 136, New York, NY 10016

Library of Congress Cataloging-in-Publication Data

Names: Best, Arthur, author.
Title: A hermit crab's shell / Arthur Best.
Description: First edition. | New York : Cavendish Square, 2019. | Series:
Animal homes | Audience: Grade K-2. | Includes index.
Identifiers: LCCN 2017048038 (print) | LCCN 2017048690 (ebook) | ISBN 9781502636584 (library bound) |
ISBN 9781502636607 (paperback) | ISBN 9781502636614 (6 pack) | ISBN 9781502636591 (ebook)
Subjects: LCSH: Hermit crabs--Juvenile literature.
Classification: LCC QL444.M33 (ebook) | LCC QL444.M33 B43 2019 (print) | DDC 595.3/87--dc23
LC record available at https://lccn.loc.gov/2017048038

Editorial Director: David McNamara
Copy Editor: Rebecca Rohan
Associate Art Director: Amy Greenan
Designer: Megan Metté
Production Coordinator: Karol Szymczuk
Photo Research: J8 Media

The photographs in this book are used by permission and through the courtesy of: Cover Antonio Luis Martinez Cano/Moment//Getty Images; p. 5 Faracowski/iStockphoto.com; p. 7 Mirco Salici/EyeEm/Getty Images; p. 9 Alex Hyde / Steve Bloom Images/Alamy Stock Photo; p. 11 Franco Banfi/WaterFrame/Getty Images; p. 13 Nino Arcutti/Alamy Stock Photo; p. 15 Comstock/Stockbyte/Thinkstock; p. 17 Pat Bonish/Alamy Stock Photo; p. 19 Paulo Oliveira/Alamy Stock Photo; p. 21 Zoonar/P.Malyshev/Zoonar/Thinkstock.com.

Printed in the United States of America

Contents

Hermit crabs are crabs.

Most live in the sea.

Some live on land.

5

A hermit crab lives in a **shell**.

7

The crab's body is soft.

The shell is hard.

The shell keeps the crab safe.

9

Hermit crabs do not grow their shells.

They use shells they find.

They can use **snail** shells.

11

A hermit crab grows.

It gets **bigger**.

The shell does not.

13

The crab gets too big!

The shell does not fit.

The crab needs a new one.

15

The crab looks for a bigger shell.

The shell must be **empty**.

The crab must fit in it.

17

The crab finds a new shell.

It will fit.

The crab **enters** its new home!

It leaves its old shell.

18

19

The crab will get bigger.

It will find a bigger shell.

The shell will fit.

That will be a new home, too!

New Words

bigger (BIG-ger) Not as small as something else.

empty (EMP-tee) Not having anything inside.

enters (EN-terz) Goes into.

shell (SHEL) A hard thing that covers some animals.

snail (SNEYL) A sea animal with a shell.

Index

About the Author

Arthur Best lives in Wisconsin with his wife and son. He has written many other books for children. He has seen a hermit crab on a beach.

About  BOOKWORMS

Bookworms help independent readers gain reading confidence through high-frequency words, simple sentences, and strong picture/text support. Each book explores a concept that helps children relate what they read to the world they live in.